Australian Firefighters

Aaron White

www.childrensbooksbyaaronwhite.com
www.facebook.com/childrensbooksbyaaronwhite

DEDICATION

I dedicate this book to my beautiful wife Francesca, my wonderful son, Tyler and to all of the Awesome Australian Firefighters. You men and women do such a fantastic job, and I hope this book helps to teach people more about the great machines and equipment that we use to fight fires.

Copyright © 2017 Aaron White
All rights reserved.

ISBN-13: 978-0-9943915-6-8

SPECIAL THANKS

To DFES and Secret Harbour Fire and Rescue for allowing us to come down to their station and take the fantastic photos needed to make this great book. Also a special thanks to Callum White for taking these photos.

Hi! I'm Aaron, and I am a qualified Australian Firefighter. Come along with me, and I will show you some of the Awesome Machines and Equipment that we use to put out fires and save people's lives and houses.

First off, we have to protect ourselves. So, I wear a helmet with a visor to protect my head and face. For my body, I have a special fire jacket and pants. I also have gloves for my hands; and for my feet, I have steel cap boots.

Here is Luke, the Firefighter. He is wearing a Breathing Apparatus set or a BA set. This set allows him to breathe clean air out of the cylinder on his back. This is important for when we go into smoky areas such as a burning building.

This is our Light Tanker. On its back is a fast attack line, which is a hose and a pump, attached to a small water tank. If we see a fire, we can stop, start up the pump and be putting water on the fire in less than 2 minutes. Now that is fast!

We use Helicopters that have water tanks fitted to their base. The Helicopters are used to drop water onto the fires that are hard to reach with our fire trucks. They refill their tanks by using a long suction hose that the pilot lowers into a dam.

This is a Fire Extinguisher. We use these to put out small fires such as the ones in a car or at a shopping centre. They are a lot lighter and easier to carry than a hose full of water. Just aim the black hose at the fire and squeeze the trigger.

Here we have the Spreaders and Cutters. If there has been a car accident and there is someone stuck in the car, both of these can be used to cut the door or the roof off to get the person out. The Spreaders are also called the "Jaws of Life".

Here we have the Control Panel. We turn this on to get the water into the hose. Also in my hands, I have the Branch. To make the water come out of the Branch and onto the fire, I just pull this lever back and aim it at the fire.

This is our Red Fire and Rescue Truck. It has a big water tank with a hose attached to it for fighting fires. It also has lots of lockers filled with rescue equipment, such as the Spreaders and Cutters, and the BA sets.

For bush fires, we use our White Fire Trucks. Their lockers are full of bush firefighting equipment like suction hoses, which are used to suck water out of a dam to refill the fire truck. It is also a four-wheel drive, so it can go up steep hills.

We use Fire Hydrants to refill the fire trucks. We do this by connecting a big red fire hose from the Fire Hydrant to the fire truck. Then we turn it on, just like a big tap.

I hope that you have had lots of fun learning about all of these Awesome Firefighting Machines and Equipment.

I have left some blank pages for you to draw your favourite machines and equipment on.

www.ingramcontent.com/pod-product-compliance
Lightning Source LLC
Chambersburg PA
CBHW041437010526
44118CB00002B/108